TAYLOR SWIFT and PAUL MCCARTNEY

Legendary Songwriters

Tim Cooke

Lerner Publications ◆ Minneapolis

Lerner Publications Company
An imprint of Lerner Publishing Group, Inc.
241 First Avenue North
Minneapolis, MN 55401 USA

For reading levels and more information, look up this title at www.lernerbooks.com.

Main body text set in Eurostile LT Pro.
Typeface provided by Linotype.

Library of Congress Cataloging-in-Publication Data

Names: Cooke, Tim, 1961- author.
Title: Taylor Swift and Paul McCartney : legendary songwriters / Tim Cooke.
Description: Minneapolis : Lerner Publications, 2024. | Series: Musicians and their inspirations | Includes bibliographical references and index. | Audience: Ages 8-12 | Audience: Grades 4-6 | Summary: "Taylor Swift grew up with Paul McCartney as her inspiration. But it goes both ways. McCartney considers Swift an inspiration too. Young readers learn more about their craft, influences on each other, music, and more"—Provided by publisher.
Identifiers: LCCN 2023046317 (print) | LCCN 2023046318 (ebook) | ISBN 9798765626726 (library binding) | ISBN 9798765629130 (paperback) | ISBN 9798765635841 (epub)
Subjects: LCSH: Swift, Taylor, 1989-—Juvenile literature. | McCartney, Paul—Juvenile literature. | Singers—Biography—Juvenile literature. | Musicians—Biography—Juvenile literature.
Classification: LCC ML3930.S989 C66 2024 (print) | LCC ML3930.S989 (ebook) | DDC 782.42164092/2 [B]—dc23/eng/20231003

LC record available at https://lccn.loc.gov/2023046317
LC ebook record available at https://lccn.loc.gov/2023046318

Manufactured in the United States of America

1 - CG - 7/15/24

TABLE OF CONTENTS

Introduction

At every concert during her 2023 Eras world tour, Taylor Swift performed her huge hit "Lover." While she sang the song, Swift played her bass guitar. She calls the guitar "Paul's bass." The instrument is similar to the bass guitar played by her hero and inspiration, Paul McCartney.

Taylor Swift plays guitar during a 2012 performance in London, England.

When Swift wrote "Lover" in 2019, she often thought about the older musician. She asked herself what McCartney would do. For more than sixty years, McCartney has put his thoughts and feelings into his songs. Swift also uses her songs to explore how she feels about her life. Just like McCartney, Swift taught herself how to play music, sing, and write songs.

Paul McCartney performs in 2018 in Austin, Texas.

Although they both rose to astronomical fame, McCartney and Swift started out on very different paths. But what they shared was a drive and love for music.

McCartney grew up with music. His dad played jazz music. McCartney taught himself how to play the piano and bass guitar. There was always music at home. In 1956, McCartney's mother died. The next year, a fifteen-year-old McCartney joined a band named the Quarrymen. His friend, John Lennon, had started the band in Liverpool, England, and invited him to join.

McCartney was already a songwriter. He began writing for the group with Lennon. After an accident took away the life of Lennon's mom, McCartney and Lennon grew closer over the grief of losing their mothers at a young age.

McCartney (above) and Lennon (right) were the main songwriters for the Beatles (below).

In 1960, the Quarrymen changed their name to the Beatles. For the next ten years, the Beatles were the most famous band in the world, putting out hit after hit. After the band split in 1970, McCartney had another successful band named Wings. He later became a solo artist. He released hit albums such as *Driving Rain*, *Memory Almost Full*, and *Egypt Station*.

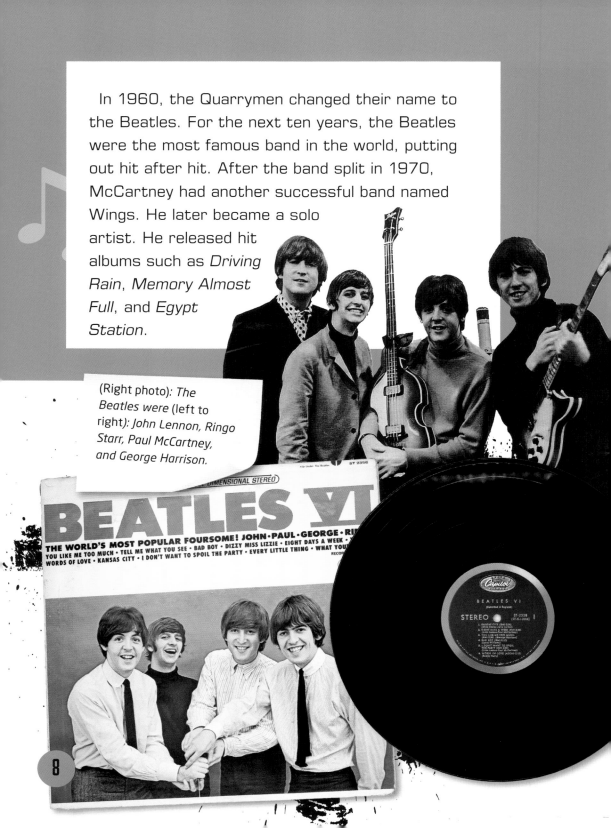

(Right photo)*: The Beatles were (left to right): John Lennon, Ringo Starr, Paul McCartney, and George Harrison.*

DIMENSIONAL STEREO

BEATLES VI

THE WORLD'S MOST POPULAR FOURSOME! JOHN · PAUL · GEORGE · RI

YOU LIKE ME TOO MUCH · TELL ME WHAT YOU SEE · BAD BOY · DIZZY MISS LIZZIE · EIGHT DAYS A WEEK ·
WORDS OF LOVE · KANSAS CITY · I DON'T WANT TO SPOIL THE PARTY · EVERY LITTLE THING · WHAT YOU

ST 2358

Country Roots

Swift learned to sing at an early age. When she was just eleven years old, she sang the national anthem at a Philadelphia 76ers basketball game. The following year, she taught herself to play the guitar and started to write her own songs. Her early inspirations were country singers such as Shania Twain and the Chicks.

Swift plays an acoustic guitar decorated with rhinestones gifted by her parents.

Swift's whole family moved to Nashville, Tennessee, when she was thirteen. The city was the center of the country music industry. The move paid off for Swift's career. In 2004, at the age of fourteen, she signed a deal with a music publisher to become a songwriter. This gave her the chance to work with more experienced songwriters.

Singing Star

Sometimes Swift performed her own songs at venues. On one of those occasions, a record executive heard her sing. He signed her on as a singer. In 2006, Swift released her first single, "Tim McGraw." She was just sixteen, but she was already very ambitious. As she said of herself, "I'm intimidated by the fear of being average."

Taylor Swift appears on NBC's Today Show in 2010.

INSPIRING THE INSPIRATION

LITTLE RICHARD

McCartney's idol was Black US singer and songwriter, Little Richard. Little Richard was a rock and roll star in the 1950s. His songs, such as "Tutti Frutti" and "Good Golly Miss Molly," were hugely popular. Early in McCartney's career, the Beatles appeared as the opening act for one of Little Richard's concerts.

11

CHAPTER 2

Writing Hits

Swift and McCartney are both successful songwriters. Between them, they have written some of the most popular songs of the last decades.

All songwriters have different methods of songwriting. McCartney had his own routine. "I never wrote words first, it was always some kind of accompaniment," he said. One song where he wrote the words first was the Beatles' hit "All My Loving." After McCartney wrote the words, he figured out the melody on a piano backstage at a concert.

McCartney often starts off with an idea such as a phrase or tune and starts playing with it. He says, "Usually I'll sit down, and I'll start something I fancy doing . . . [and I see] where it leads me."

McCartney has worked with famous artists such as Stevie Wonder (right).

Three Types of Lyrics

For many people, songwriting is all about the melody. But for Swift, her favorite part of songwriting is writing lyrics. She divides her lyrics into three different styles: Quill Lyrics, Fountain Pen Lyrics, and Glitter Gel Pen Lyrics.

Quill Lyrics read like old poetry. Swift finds inspiration for them after reading work by writers such as Charlotte Brontë and Emily Dickinson. Fountain Pen Lyrics are about modern stories of love and loss. Glitter Gel Pen Lyrics are lyrics that don't take life too seriously. They're meant to just be fun.

Swift's piano is decorated with the name of her 2017 album, Reputation.

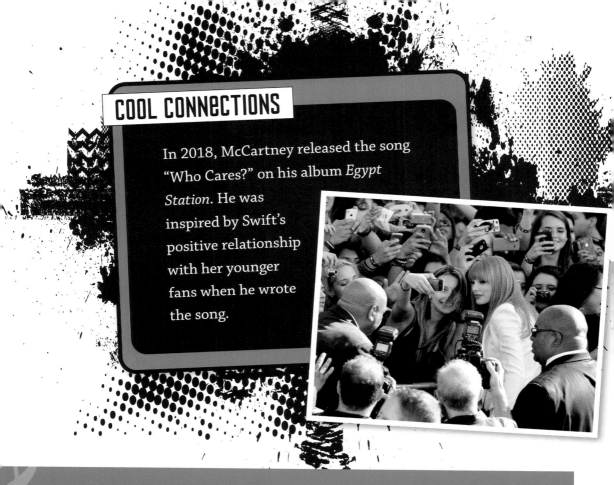

Swift doesn't always start by writing lyrics. But once she has her lyrics, she finds the melody to go with it. Sometimes songs come to her at night in a dream. When she wakes up, she records the song so she doesn't forget it. Then she works on it later. She also co-writes songs with other singers.

CHAPTER 3

Sold Out!

Fans adore McCartney's and Swift's live performances. When these singers are on stage, they deliver their best!

McCartney has played thousands of gigs since the 1960s. He's played at some of the biggest stadiums in the world. In 1990, he played in front of 184,000 fans at the Maracaña Stadium in Rio de Janeiro, Brazil. But McCartney doesn't only play huge stadiums. In 2022, he performed in front of just eight hundred fans in Somerset, England.

Changing Appearances

When McCartney was still with the Beatles, their sets often lasted only thirty minutes. The rest of the time would be filled up by other acts. The Beatles were known for wearing suits on stage and playing as a band.

McCartney wears colorful clothes on stage so he stands out from his band members.

At the start of their career, the Beatles often wore identical suits.

McCartney has played to huge audiences around the world.

In 2022, McCartney's solo appearances lasted almost three hours. He wore simple clothes: jackets, shirts, and waistcoats. He would play old Beatles hits, as well as his latest songs. Fans loved seeing the living legend in person.

Changing Shows

Swift's shows went on even longer than McCartney's. In March 2023, she started her year-long Eras world tour. The concerts lasted over three hours. She played more than forty songs at each concert.

Swift changed her costumes constantly on stage. She wore clothes from sequined bodysuits to glamorous evening gowns. Huge sets covered the stage. These changed every few songs to reflect the different mood of each of her ten albums. One was a cabin covered in moss. Another had a swimming pool. Her concerts were like theater performances.

Swift plans her stage sets and wardrobes to create the best show for the audience.

Swift might change her stage clothes up to sixteen times during a single concert.

Breaking Records

The Eras Tour broke many records. It was the first tour in history to earn over a billion dollars. It sold more than a million tickets worldwide. So many fans tried to buy tickets that Ticketmaster, a site fans use to buy concert tickets, went into meltdown. Swift herself was amazed by her success. "I figured it would be fun, but I did not know it would be like this," she said.

COOL CONNECTIONS

McCartney and Swift have each performed a world tour with more than one hundred concerts. The Paul McCartney World Tour lasted 108 concerts. Swift's Eras Tour was more than 140 concerts.

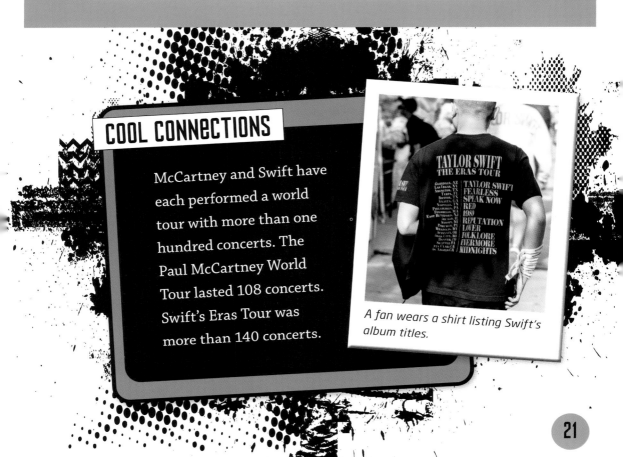

A fan wears a shirt listing Swift's album titles.

CHAPTER 4

Award-Winning Artists

McCartney is quite late in his career. Swift has been in the industry since she was a teenager and shows no signs of stopping. They both share one thing: huge personal success.

McCartney is one of the most successful musicians of all time. His career has lasted more than sixty years. In 1988, he was inducted into the Rock and Roll Hall of Fame as a Beatle. Then he was inducted into it in 1999 as a solo artist. In 1997, Queen Elizabeth knighted him for his accomplishments in music. Over his career, he has won eighteen Grammy Awards. He has sold millions of albums and earned sixty gold records.

McCartney was awarded a star on the Hollywood Walk of Fame in 2012.

PAUL MC CARTNEY

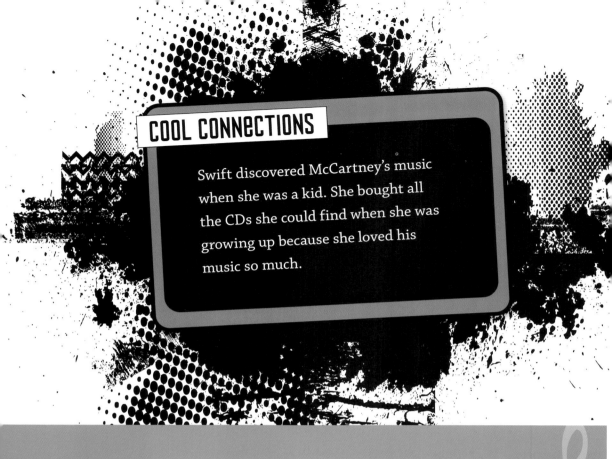

COOL CONNECTIONS

Swift discovered McCartney's music when she was a kid. She bought all the CDs she could find when she was growing up because she loved his music so much.

Despite his success, McCartney never stopped writing or making music. After the Beatles split up in 1970, McCartney's albums have all charted in the *Billboard* 100. His band Wings had fourteen top ten singles in the US charts. As a solo artist, he has continued to record and perform.

Record Breaker

Since the day she began performing, Swift has smashed record after record. Her Eras world tour broke the record for most earnings, surpassing over one billion dollars. In the summer of 2023, she became the most streamed female artist on Spotify, with 100 million monthly listeners. She tied the record for most wins at the Video Music Awards in 2023. She took home eight awards, including Artist of the Year.

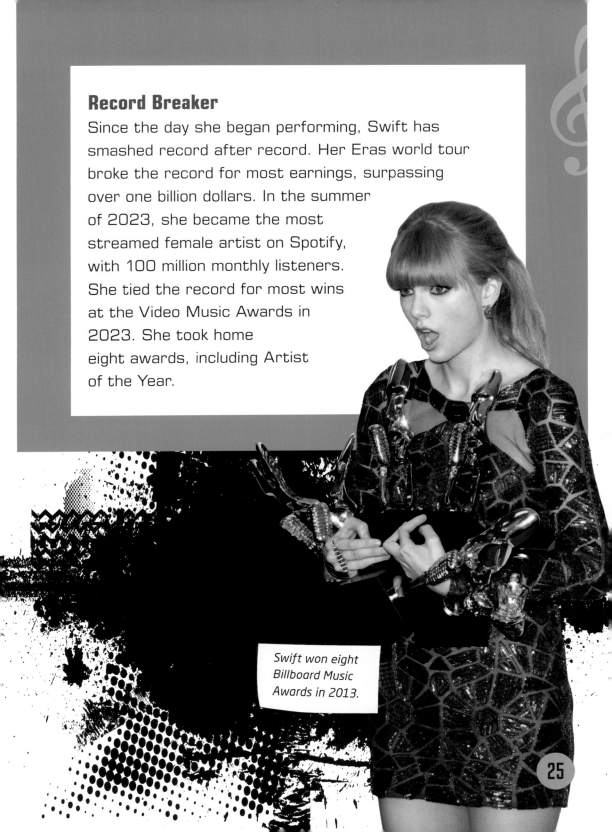

Swift won eight Billboard Music Awards in 2013.

Fans celebrate Swift's favorite number, 13.

Fans' Friend

Swift is not just popular for her songs. She loves and gives back to her fans, who are known as "Swifties." They see her as a role model. "Fans are my favorite thing in the world," she says. "I've never been the type of artist who has that line drawn between their friends and their fans."

Your Inspiration

Paul McCartney has been a star for more than sixty years. In that time, he has achieved large success with his bands and as a solo artist. But he also gives back to the community. He donates to causes such as the Humane Society and Elton John AIDS Foundation.

McCartney was a role model for Taylor Swift. Swift has used her fame to bond with her fans and give back. She is an active supporter of the Make-a-Wish Foundation. She also encourages her fans, especially young girls, to be confident in themselves.

Who inspires you? They don't have to be someone famous. It could be anyone: your best friend, your teacher, your aunt, or a person in your community. Why do they inspire you? What can you learn from them?

IMPORTANT DATES

1957 — Paul McCartney joins John Lennon's band, the Quarrymen.

1960 — The Quarrymen change their name to the Beatles. They become the biggest band in the world.

1970 — The Beatles split up. McCartney starts a solo career and forms the band Wings.

1997 — The Queen knights McCartney for his services to music.

2004 — Taylor Swift signs to Sony/ATV as a songwriter.

2006 — Swift releases her first single, "Tim McGraw."

2020 — Swift releases her eighth album, *Folklore*.

2023 — Swift becomes the most streamed monthly female artist on Spotify.

2024 — Swift's record-breaking Eras Tour comes to an end.

GLOSSARY

accompaniment: music played along with a solo part, either vocal or instrumental

bass guitar: a guitar that produces low tones

country: a form of popular music that began in the southern US and includes ballads and dance tunes

Covid-19: an infectious disease that impacted most of the globe beginning in 2020

Grammy: an award given to artists for their achievements in music

idol: a person who is loved and admired for their accomplishments

lyric: the words to a song

melody: an arrangement of musical notes that makes a tune

solo: performing alone

stream: to listen to music directly from the internet

venue: the place where an event is held

SOURCE NOTES

10   Laura Snapes, "Taylor Swift's Reputation: Will Her New Album Silence Her Critics?" *Guardian*, November 9, 2017, https://www.theguardian.com/music/2017/nov/09/taylor-swift-reputation-can-new-album-save-her-name.

12   Sam Kemp, "The Song That Changed How Paul McCartney Wrote Music," *Far Out*, March 25, 2023, https://faroutmagazine.co.uk/song-that-changed-paul-mccartney-songwritng-appraoch/.

12   Sam Kemp, "Paul McCartney Reveals His Secret Songwriting Tips," *Far Out*, December 21, 2021, https://faroutmagazine.co.uk/paul-mccartney-secret-songwriting-tips/.

21   Jeannie Kopstein and Mariah Espada, "The Staggering Econonic Impact of Taylor Swift's Eras Tour," *Time*, updated August 24, 2023, https://time.com/6307420/taylor-swift-eras-tour-money-economy/

26   Kara Johnson, "The Importance of Taylor Swift's Relationship with her Fans," Fansided, updated October 18, 2017, https://culturess.com/2017/10/18/the-importance-of-taylor-swifts-relationship-with-her-fans/.

LEARN MORE

Britannica Kids: Paul McCartney
https://kids.britannica.com/students/article/Paul-McCartney/312411

Britannica Kids: Taylor Swift
https://kids.britannica.com/students/article/Taylor-Swift/487625

Britannica Kids: The Beatles
https://kids.britannica.com/kids/article/the-Beatles/390013

Cooke, Tim. *Harry Styles and Mick Jagger: Music and Style Icons.*
Minneapolis: Lerner Publications, 2025.

Huddleston, Emma. *Taylor Swift.* Lake Elmo, MN: Focus Readers, 2021.

Kawa, Katie. *Taylor Swift: Making a Difference as a Songwriter.* New
York: KidHaven Publishing, 2022.

Kiddle: Paul McCartney Facts for Kids
https://kids.kiddle.co/Paul_McCartney

Kiddle: Taylor Swift Facts for Kids
https://kids.kiddle.co/Taylor_Swift

INDEX

PHOTO ACKNOWLEDGMENTS

Image credits: Featureflash/Dreamstime.com, p. 4; Raph_PH/Wikimedia Commons, p. 5; Chris Dorney/ Dreamstime.com, p. 7a; meunierd/Shutterstock.com, p. 7b; EMI/Billboard/Wikimedia Commons, p. 8a; Blueee77/Shutterstock.com, p. 8b; Debby Wong/Shutterstock.com, pp. 9, 10; Skyhawk/Shutterstock. com, p. 11a Gyvafoto/Shutterstock.com, p. 11b Globe Poster Baltimore/Live Auctioneers.com/ Wikimedia Commons, p. 11c; Jim Summaria/Wikimedia Commons, p.13a; Samantha Appleton/The White House/Wikimedia Commons, p. 13b; Dvmsimages/Dreamstime.com, p. 14a; Deelu9/Dreamstime. com, p. 14b; Luke Richardson/Dreamstime.com, p. 14c; Ronald Woan/Wikimedia Commons, pp. 14d, 20b, 20c; Featureflash Photo Agency/Shutterstock.com, p. 15; Jaroslav Noska/Dreamstime.com, p. 17a; Shutterstock/Shutterstock Editorial, p. 17b; Aliaksandr Mazurkevich /Dreamstime.com, p. 18a; Pete Souza/The White House/Wikimedia Commons, p. 18b; Paolo Villanueva/Wikimedia Commons, p. 19a; Christian Bertrand/Shutterstock.com, p. 19b; Zana Zills/Wikimedia Commons, p. 20a; ezellhphotography/Shutterstock.com, p. 21; Carrienelson1/Dreamstime.com, p. 23a; Biansho/ Dreamstime.com, p. 23b; s_bukley/Shutterstock.com, pp. 25, 26b. Wilson0204/Wikimedia Commons, p.26a. Cover: Paolo Villanueva/Wikimedia Commons; D Wong/Shutterstock.com.